James Finley Weir Johnston

The Suspending Power and the Writ of Habeas Corpus

James Finley Weir Johnston

The Suspending Power and the Writ of Habeas Corpus

ISBN/EAN: 9783744732079

Printed in Europe, USA, Canada, Australia, Japan

Cover: Foto ©ninafisch / pixelio.de

More available books at **www.hansebooks.com**

THE

SUSPENDING POWER

AND

The Writ

OF

HABEAS CORPUS.

PHILADELPHIA:

JOHN CAMPBELL, BOOKSELLER,

419 CHESTNUT STREET.

1862.

Suspending Power and the Writ of Habeas Corpus.

THE people of the United States, through State Conventions, ordained that the Constitution should be the supreme law of the land; and to secure the blessings of liberty to themselves and their posterity, by the 1st clause of the 9th section of the 1st Article, declared that

"The privilege of the Writ of *Habeas Corpus* shall not be suspended, unless when, in cases of rebellion or invasion, the public safety may require it."

It will be observed that this does not, nor does the Constitution elsewhere, *grant* this privilege to the people. It assumes that they have it.

It *prohibits* the Government of the United States, and all its departments, under any and all circumstances, from totally *depriving* the people of this, their privilege; but it does grant the power to *suspend* that privilege when, but not till, two things shall concur and have been determined by the competent authority, viz:

1. A rebellion, (*or* an invasion,) and

2. That the public *safety requires* it to be then suspended.

This clause grants, that, under these concurring conditions, that power may be exercised by—*whom?* That is the inquiry.

It is affirmed by some, that that power is granted to the *President*, and by others that it belongs to the *Congress*. No one has thus far contended that it belongs to *each* of them, nor yet to the *Judiciary*. It follows that the power can be exercised only by the Congress *or* by the President.

For the President's power it has been said:

I. That the phrases, "privilege of the Writ," and "suspended" as predicated of that privilege, are expressions unknown to the common or to parliamentary law—and that "suspending the Habeas Corpus Act" is an "inaccurate expression," as the *Act* "was never for a moment suspended." That "suspending the privilege"

(3)

was a phrase "*first* used in the Constitution of the United States," hence all analogy from the English law and Constitution must be discarded.

II. That a temporary denial of the privilege by a single act (founded on the authority of the Constitution) is all that is necessary to suspend the privilege. And as this power to deny (temporarily) a discharge "is an executive power," therefore to suspend the privilege is an executive power.

III. That all the conditions of the exercise of the power (to suspend), that is to say, rebellion or invasion, and the requirement of the public safety in the time of either, are of executive and not of legislative cognizance. And as the power (of suspension) can only be exercised by that department which can take this cognizance, therefore the Executive only can exercise it.

IV. That the only thing required for the exercise of this power to suspend, (given the conditions,) is an authority above the law which gives or may give the Writ; but *that* authority is in this clause of the Constitution *itself*, therefore a legislative power is not required; and as the framers of the Constitution did not give the power to a department not required to exercise it, hence they did not give it to Congress.

V. That this power, (to be exercised only in case of internal war, viz., rebellion or invasion,) necessarily belongs to him only whose duty it is to put down the war, (*i. e.*, rebellion,) but it is the duty of the President (*only?*) to suppress rebellion, therefore, this power to suspend the privilege belongs to him only.

VI. Congress, by any law it might pass, could only grant an authority to the President to suspend, but that authority has already been given (to the President?) by the Constitution; therefore their law would be useless, and as the framers of the Constitution can not be supposed to have authorized Congress to do a useless act, hence they did not give this power to Congress.

A gentleman, of Philadelphia, of high legal reputation, has published an argument to prove that the Convention which prepared the Constitution of the United States, meant to give to the *President*, and *not* to *Congress*, the power to suspend the *privilege* of the Habeas Corpus. These propositions are the pith of his argument, and it is in reply to them that the following remarks are submitted.

In considering this subject there are certain things to be constantly kept in mind. They are,

1. That it is *not* the question whether the Government or any of its departments would, in a time of extreme peril, be excusable for suspending the Habeas Corpus, or arresting upon suspicion, or for doing any other act, *not warranted* by the *Constitution*, but which the public safety might require.

2. It is *not* a question about the power of the General Government, or what *it* may or may *not* do.

3. The question *is*—to which of two of the departments, viz., the Executive or the Congress, did the framers of the Constitution *mean* to give the power?

4. *We* may think that, upon every ground of reason and fitness, the President alone ought to have the power; but if the authors of this Constitution did not give it to him, then we dare not say he has it.

5. In seeking for their meaning we must look at the subject, not from our own, but from their point of view. Through what medium did they look at it? It was doubtless a very different one from the present, but it is nevertheless the only one through which we should view it.

The clause itself has already been quoted. It has correctly been said that the sentence is elliptical; but that it may be read with the proper ellipsis, and show more clearly the sense ascribed to it, by those who argue for the President's power of suspension, let it be written thus, viz:

"The privilege of the Writ of Habeas Corpus shall not be suspended, unless when, in cases of rebellion or invasion, the public safety may require it;" [*and then the President may suspend it.*]

Those who contend that the power of suspension is in the President, do and must read that section as it is thus written; while those who affirm that the power is in Congress alone, must substitute *the Congress* for *the President*.

The history of the clause has been stated with conciseness and accuracy, but as it will be referred to in the following remarks, a re-statement of it, with one or two additional facts, may aid in its interpretation.

When the Convention was ready to proceed to business, Mr. Edmund Randolph, of Virginia, offered fifteen resolutions, as the basis of a plan, and Mr. Charles Pinckney, of South Carolina, offered, as the plan of the Federal Government, sixteen articles.

Mr. Randolph meant by his propositions merely to introduce other and more particular ones, which would explain the outlines of the system he had in view.

The plan of Mr. Pinckney seemed designed as a complete Constitution; and, in its general tenor and form, it very much resembled the Constitution afterwards adopted.

Article VI. related to the *Legislature* of the United States, and in it were grouped nearly all the powers given to, and the restrictions upon, that department; after an enumeration of the several powers so given, it contained this clause:

"The *Legislature* of the United States shall pass no law on the subject of religion, nor touching or abridging the liberty of the press; *nor shall the privilege of the Writ of Habeas Corpus ever be suspended except in case of rebellion or invasion.*"

With the exception of Mr. Patterson's plan, which was offered on the 15th and rejected on the 19th of June, those of Mr. Randolph and Mr. Pinckney, were the only ones offered. The Convention, with those two plans before it, resolved itself into a Committee of the Whole House, and then took up Mr. Randolph's fifteen resolutions, which, one by one, they debated and amended, till the fifteenth of June, when the Committee reported to the Convention nineteen resolutions, based on Mr. Randolph's plan. These were debated till July 26, when all their proceedings (except those relating to the National Executive, which they retained for debate) were, together with the plan of Mr. Pinckney and the resolutions of Mr. Patterson, referred to a Committee of five, or of detail, who, on August 5, reported to the Convention a plan of a Constitution, containing twenty-three articles. In the VIIth of these were classed the powers given to, and the restrictions upon, the *Legislature*, in like manner as in the plan of Mr. Pinckney.

Art. XI. related to the *Judiciary*, and the 4th section of it was as follows:—" Sec. 4.—The trial of all criminal offences (except in case of impeachment) shall be in the State *where* they shall be committed, and shall be by jury."

Other resolutions were from time to time afterwards referred to the Committee of Detail, but in this, their first report, there was no clause relating to the *Habeas Corpus*.

On the 20th of August, Mr. Pinckney submitted and the House referred to the Committee of Detail, certain propositions, one of which was this, viz :—

" The privileges and benefit of the writ of *Habeas Corpus* shall be enjoyed in this *Government* in the most expeditious and ample manner, and shall not be suspended by the *Legislature*, except upon the most urgent and pressing occasions, and for a limited time, not exceeding —— months."—Mad. Deb., 5. Ell. Deb., p. 484.

This was the second time that Mr. Pinckney had, among other resolutions, offered one restraining the suspension of the privilege of the Habeas Corpus, and on the 28th of August, and when Sec. 4 of Article XI., relating to the *Judiciary*, was under discussion, it was amended, *nem. con.*, so as to read:

" Sec. 4.—The trial of all crimes (except in cases of impeachment) shall be by jury; and such trial shall be held in the State *where* the said crimes shall have been committed; but when not committed within any State, then the trial shall be at such place or places as the Legislature may direct."

Mr. Madison (5 Ell. Deb., p. 484) immediately adds,—" Mr. Pinckney, urging the propriety of securing the benefit of the Habeas Corpus in the most ample manner, moved that it should not be suspended but on the most urgent occasions, and then only for a limited time, not exceeding twelve months.

" Mr. Rutledge was for declaring the *Habeas Corpus inviolable.* He did not conceive that a suspension could ever be necessary at the *same time*, through *all the States.*"

" Mr. Governeur Morris moved that " The privilege of the writ of Habeas Corpus shall not be suspended, unless *where*, in cases of rebellion or invasion, the public safety may require it."

" Mr. Wilson doubted whether in any case a suspension could be necessary, as the discretion now exists with the judges in the most important cases to keep in gaol or admit to bail."

The first part of Mr. Governeur Morris's motion, to the word " unless," was agreed to, *nem. con.*

On the remaining part—New Hampshire, Massachusetts, Connecticut, Pennsylvania, Delaware, Maryland, Virginia,—7 voted aye; North Carolina, South Carolina, Georgia,—3 voted no. So this clause was, as it is expressed on the journal, "added" to the 4th section. It will be observed that in place of the word *"when"* which is now in the Constitution, Mr. Morris used, and the Convention adopted, the word *"where."* This was an amendment to a section which provided for the place *where* trials should be held, and it may be that Mr. Morris intended by the word " where" to limit the suspension of the writ to the *place* where, in cases of rebellion or invasion, the public safety might require it to be suspended. Confirmatory of this are the words of Mr. Rutledge, which, briefly as they are reported, show that he did not think " that a suspension could ever be necessary, at the same time, *through all* the States"— but only, of course, in a *part* of them ; and immediately *after* this, Mr. Morris moved the foregoing clause. A little reflection must have convinced him, however, that the discretion given to the suspending power by the latter words of the clause, would allow it to be suspended at the same time through all the States," quite as well with " where" as with " when ;" hence *if* the clause properly related to the *Legislature,* then the mover of it, and who, as the Chairman of the Committee on Style and Arrangement, *changed* this amendment from the XIth Article, which related to the *Judiciary,* to the IXth Article, which related to the *Legislature,* would very naturally and probably substitute "when" for "where." That the words were changed is not denied; it does not appear that the *Convention* made the change, and it is therefore probable that Mr. Morris himself did it. The reason first assigned, and its influence upon the meaning of the clause, will be hereafter noticed.

Thus being made a part of the supreme law of the land, is this power of suspension in the President, *or* in the Legislature ?

In the first place it has been said that " this is a political rather than a legal question,—a *mixed* political and Constitutional question." And what then ? Does that render the question itself easier of solution ? Call it what you will, it still recurs for an answer. What is the meaning of the clause ?

Doubtless here, as elsewhere, law may be divided into that part which classifies and regulates the powers of the departments of a

State, considered as a body politic, and that which regulates the conduct of the citizens of the State; and questions which relate to the former you may call *political* questions.

But what if you have not yet classified the powers of the former, or do not even know whether such departments possess a certain power, or to which one of two departments it belongs? There must be some one tribunal to determine whether the power exists, and if so where it is lodged. Let the case be that a citizen who has been imprisoned by the mere order of the President obtains a Writ of Habeas Corpus, and his keeper in the fort or prison returns that the President has suspended the privilege of the Writ, and has ordered the detention of the prisoner, the question thus presented is, can the *President* suspend the privilege of that writ?

Is that rather a political than a legal question? or is it not the latter only, and one which the Judiciary alone can decide? It would seem that simply to state such a case would be to answer it affirmatively. Judge Washington said of a like question—"This question does not so much involve a contest for *power* between (two departments of the Government) as the rights and *privileges* of the citizen secured to him by the Constitution, the benefit of which he may justly claim."—5 Wheat. Rep., 22. And more than forty years ago, Mr. Webster, in replying to a similar remark, said, in the Convention to amend the Constitution of Massachusetts, "We look to the judicial tribunal for protection against illegal or unconstitutional acts, from whatever quarter they may proceed. It is the theory and plan of the Constitution to restrain the Legislature as well as other departments, and to subject their acts to judicial decision, whenever it appears that such acts infringe constitutional limits—and without this check, no certain limitation could exist on the exercise of legislative power. The Constitution, for example, declares that the Legislature shall not suspend the privilege or benefit of the Writ of *Habeas Corpus*, except under certain limitations. If a law should happen to be passed, restraining personal liberty, and an individual, feeling oppressed by it, should apply for his *Habeas Corpus*, must not the judges decide what *is* the *benefit* of the *Habeas Corpus* intended by the Constitution; what it is to *suspend it*, and whether the act of the Legislature does, in the given case, conform to the Constitution? All these questions would of course arise."

"It is a rule in construing treaties," and a much stronger one in construing a Constitution, "that, from history and policy, as well as language, are to be gathered the views of the parties making them." —Johnson, J., 6 Wheat. 85. By the common law of England, every freeman had the absolute and unqualified right to the liberty of his person. To suppose that right, without the legal means of maintaining it, or of regaining it, would be the highest absurdity; therefore, by the law he was entitled to be forthwith restored to his liberty; but as he might have violated the law, and, therefore, his liberty be rightly restrained, the duly constituted *Judges* were commanded to *inquire* and determine whether he had done so or not, and as that could only be done by legal process or writ, it follows that such writ must necessarily result from, and be coeval with, the right itself; the party imprisoned was thus of *right* entitled to the writ; which is, therefore, called by the common law a writ *of right*. It was not one, the granting of which depended on the favor of the King, or the discretion of the Judges, for that would have been to make his will or their discretion the measure of the people's rights.

At the common law, even in the reign of King Alfred, the most ancient book in the law says there was no such thing as a writ of favor, for they were all remedial writs, grantable *as of debt*, as due of right.—(Mirror of Justice; c. 5, s. 1.)*

That the common law did not allow the people to be imprisoned at the mere will of the King, and that they had a right to be forthwith released from such imprisonment, did not hinder the Kings of England from beating down the right, or delaying the remedy.

From the time that King John ascended the throne, till James II. abdicated, there was an undying struggle between the prerogative to imprison without bail, trial, or judgment, and the privilege from arrest, unless by due course of law.

The ignorance and wilful disregard, by King John and his Judges, of the old and accustomed laws and rights of the people, the domestic injuries received from him in person, as well as from acts of

* "The Rights and Liberties of Englishmen."

general oppression, obliged them by force of arms to wrest from him the Great Charter. What those chief and accustomed laws were, and how they had been violated, may be learned from the Charter itself, and from the articles which they compelled him to subscribe to immediately preceding it.

One of those articles shortly and forcibly expresses the right of every freeman to his personal liberty, and forever forbids his imprisonment without due process of law.—Chap. 29. "Ne corpus liberi hominis capiatur nec imprisonetur nec dissaisietur nec utlagetur nec exuletur nec aliquo modo destruatur nec rex eat vel mittat super eum vi nisi per judicium parium suorum vel per legem terre."

The like words are in the Great Charter itself. But neither John nor many of his successors appear to have regarded the most solemn laws, their own Charters, or even their own oaths.

From the granting of Magna Charta till the time of Sir Edward Coke, he declared that it had been established, confirmed, and commanded to be put in execution, by two and thirty several acts of Parliament. But history has never been able to record the un. numbered violations of that Charter, especially of its prohibition of arbitrary imprisonment.

Among the devices to evade the privilege of the Habeas Corpus, and to maintain the power of arbitrary imprisonment, it was pretended that in the towers and castles of the King freemen might be imprisoned by the order of the King and his chief officers, as if those forts were not within a county, or as if the Writ of Habeas Corpus did not run therein ; but to remedy that, even in the reign of one of the most lawless and law-suspending Kings, Richard II., it was enacted that the King's castles and gaols, which were wont to be joined to the bodies of the counties, but were then severed therefrom, should be re-joined to the same counties. So intent were the people to secure their liberties entire and inviolate, that they added to the resolves of the Parliament the sanctions of the Church and of religion ; for by the fourth chapter of the Great Charter of Edward I., the archbishops and bishops were commanded to excommunicate all those who, by word, deed, or counsel, broke that or the prior Charters ; and the clergy proposed a formal and dreadful curse upon whomsoever should violate that, as in like manner in

May, 1253, the prelates of England had denounced whomsoever should break or judge against the Great Charter of Henry III.

In the Petition of Right, 3 Charles I., Chap. 1., which was presented in 1628, it was stated that the people had oaths administered to them not warranted by the laws; that Commissioners had been appointed by the King to proceed within the land, according to martial law; that when Writs of Habeas Corpus had been sued out, the prisoners were remanded to prison upon a return that they were held by the mere warrant of the King, signified through the members of his privy council; and these acts, and others of the like nature, were declared to be wholly contrary to law; and the parliament demanded, and the King, failing in his attempt to evade it, was compelled to declare that these were violations of the ancient and undoubted rights and liberties of the people, and that if the alleged offenders had violated the laws and statutes of the land, by *the same* laws and statutes also, they might, and by *no other* they *ought* to, have been judged. Even this did not restrain this King, or secure the people from arbitrary arrest. By usurpation and connivance, there had grown up a court called the *Star Chamber*, which, at first, pretended to inquire of the offences of great men and State criminals, but, on whatever pretence it was at first allowed to exercise its powers, it was soon made use of as an instrument of arbitrary power to crush whomsoever the Ministers and Secretaries of State and their favorites had a mind to put out of the way, or to destroy.

It had no known rules or laws of procedure; "Holding," as Lord Clarendon declared, " for honorable that which it pleased, and for just, that which profited." It disregarded Writs of Habeas Corpus, and its victims were left to linger in confinement.

By the 16 Charles I., c. 10, the Parliament declared that the proceedings of that Court were contrary to the rights and *privileges* of the people, an intolerable burthen, and the means to introduce an arbitrary government; and they forever abolished it. Still that did not put an end to the unlawful imprisonment of the people. For when Writs of Habeas Corpus were applied for, the judges many times pretended to have power to grant or deny the writ at their pleasure; and, when they granted them, the *jailors*, in turn, claimed, by custom, a right to keep the prisoner till a *second* and *third* Writ had been sued out, and served on them; and when the imprisoned and oppressed subject at length got the Writ, the judges would often allege that they could not release, or even take bail for his appearance to answer his accuser, *because* he was a *prisoner of State.*

To debar these and the like evasions of the people's right to the Writ, and to provide a complete and effectual remedy against its obstruction, the Parliament passed the ever memorable statute of 31 Charles the II., c. 2, known as the Habeas Corpus Act. Yet, plain and stringent as were its provisions, even that did not altogether secure the people from unlawful imprisonment; for, no sooner had James the II. ascended the throne, than he claimed the power, without the consent of Parliament, to dispense with and suspend the laws and the execution thereof.

For that claim the people drove him from his kingdom, and by the Declaration and Bill of Rights (which were declaratory only of the common law and the rights of the people) it was declared:

" I. That the pretended power of SUSPENDING laws or the *execution* of laws by Regal authority, without CONSENT OF PARLIAMENT, is illegal."

It was to avoid, among other things, the arbitrary seizure of their property and the imprisonment of their persons, without cause shown by the King or his officers of State, that the people emigrated to these Colonies.

In the Mother Country they had claimed these chartered privileges as their birth-right; but which, being refused to them there, they came here to enjoy. Those great rights being theirs, so, too, were these great remedies; in full consciousness of their right to which, they silently adopted them as their undoubted inheritance.

But as it was in England by the King, so it was here " the practice of some of the Governors to imprison the people without bail." Indeed, in their arbitrary conduct, they often exceeded that of their royal masters! Nor were the Colonial Judges behind either: witness the conduct of the Chief Justice of Massachusetts on the trial of the Rev. John Wise and others. Being denied the Writ of Habeas Corpus, they were at length put on their trial; they claimed the privileges secured to them as Englishmen by the Magna Charta and the Laws of England. The

Chief Justice, however, informed them that they must not expect "English analogies" would follow them to the ends of the earth, and concluded by telling them that they had no more privileges than to be sold as slaves.—Washbourne, Jud. Hist. Mass., 116.

And, in 1710, the Legislature of New Jersey was obliged to denounce Judge Pinham for corruptly refusing to Thomas Gordon the Writ of Habeas Corpus, which they declared was the undoubted right and great privilege of the subject.—Hurd, Habeas Corpus, p. 114. As the Revolutionary struggle drew on, the statesmen and people of this country saw clearly that it was the King who was pressing upon their privileges; they felt that his influence was great, was increasing, and would, if not checked, deprive them of their rights; and they were conscious—what history has since clearly revealed—that it was under the controlling influence of the King himself, that Lord North and his ministerial supporters passed those arbitrary and impolitic laws which drove a loyal people into rebellion.

Inspired by his will, the Ministers pressed, and had passed, the Quebec bill, which decreed an arbitrary rule over the vast region which included, besides Canada, the area of the present States of Ohio, Michigan, Indiana, Illinois, and Wisconsin. It denied the people the right of trial by jury, the Writ of Habeas Corpus, and left them to the French process of *Lettres de Cachet*, more odious than general search-warrants. This flagrant act was denounced in the several Colonies, and the Continental Congress, in September, 1774.

With the records of all history before them; with the knowledge of what their ancestors had suffered through the power which Kings and their Ministers had claimed and exercised in arresting and imprisoning the people, "that, even in the Colonies, it had been attempted to vindicate and develop the efficiency of royal proclamations, both in suspending laws already made, and in legislating for cases—not yet regulated by Statutory provisions." 1 Graham's Hist., p. 90. That they had just solemnly declared that, to their own knowledge, the King had suspended the passage of laws, and even the power of the Legislature itself, and that although these acts of the King had been done through a Legislature, yet they had been prompted by his arbitrary disposition, and carried out by his influence and will. Their own bitter experience had shown them "with how little equity absolute power is exercised even by those who have shown themselves most prompt to resent the influence of its rigor upon themselves."—1 Graham's Hist., p. 100.

Even, with their mild principles, the proprietors of Pennsylvania had lately shown that they needed but the power to play the tyrant: and Franklin, in commenting on their conduct, had just said—"*Power*, like water, is ever working its own way; and whenever it can find or make an opening, is altogether as prone to overflow whatever is subject to it. And though matters of right overlooked may be reclaimed and reassumed at any time, it cannot be too soon reclaimed and reassumed; and though protection is the reason, and consequently should be the end of government, *we ought to be as much upon our guard against our protectors* as against *our enemies*."—4 Gr. Col. Hist., p. 440. That was a period when the pulse of liberty beat high. "In other countries," said Burke, "the people, more simple, and of a less mercurial cast, judge of an ill principle in government only by an actual grievance: here they anticipate the evil, and judge of the pressure of the grievance by the badness of the principle. They augur misgovernment from a distance, and snuff the approach of tyranny in every tainted breeze."

Is it probable, then, that men, in whose minds these principles of freedom, and even of democratic freedom, were engrafted and incorporated, and who had just emerged from a struggle against the will of one man, would at once, in framing their own Government, give to one man—their Executive—a power to suspend their privileges—a power which even he, whom they had called a tyrant, could not exercise: and not only give that power, but part with it forever to him and his successors, and thus place it beyond the control of the people, or their immediate representatives?

One class of thinkers may, indeed, be predisposed to think that most probable. For what has been said of the English Constitution may, in these days, be said of our own.

"Revolution and civil war have marked the influence of opposite opinions with respect to the popular nature of our Constitution. These dreadful and perilous scenes could not fail to transmit this original division of sentiment to us—their posterity. The distinction between those who incline to the popular part of the Constitution and those who incline to the monarchial—exists to this hour, and can cease only with the Constitution itself. The great leading idea which should be formed of our constitutional history, is that there has always been a constant struggle between prerogative and privilege. * * Now, such being the real picture of our constitutional history, the student is, in the next place, to be reminded of the natural divisions, not only of mankind, but of philosophers, on political subjects and the manner in which they separate into two classes. Those, for instance, who are anxious, first and principally, for the *prerogative* of the Crown; and those, on the other hand, who are zealous, first and principally, for the *privileges* of the people."—Smythe's Lect. on Mod. Hist., p. 87, 88.

Besides, to judge correctly whether they would probably change the law in this respect, it should be considered what it then was, as finely expressed in the Commentaries of Blackstone, with which they were familiar. "Of great importance to the public is the preservation of this personal liberty; for if once it were left in the power of any, the highest magistrate, to imprison arbitrarily whomsoever he pleased or his officers thought proper, (as in France is daily practised by the Crown,) there would soon be an end of *all other rights and immunities*. Some have thought that unjust attacks even upon life or property, at the arbitrary will of the magistrate, are less dangerous to the Commonwealth, than such as are made upon the personal liberty of the subject. To bereave a man of life, or by violence to confiscate his estate without accusation or trial, would be so gross and notorious an act of despotism as must at once convey the alarm of tyranny throughout the whole kingdom; but confinement of the person, by secretly hurrying him to gaol, where his sufferings are unknown or forgotten, is a less public, a less shocking, and therefore a more dangerous engine of arbitrary government. And yet, when the State is in real danger, even this may be a necessary measure. But the *happiness of our Constitution* is, that it is *not left* to the *Executive power* to determine whether the danger of the State is so great as to render this measure expedient, [or the *public safety may require it?*] for it is the Parliament only, or the *Legislative* power, that, whenever it sees proper, can authorize the Crown, by suspending the Habeas Corpus Act for a short or limited time, to imprison without giving any reason for so doing."—1 Blk. Com., p. 135.

It was highly probable that the people of the United States would greatly limit this "Legislative power;" but if it were the happiness of the English and the American Constitutions at that time, that it was not left to the Executive to determine when the danger of the State rendered the suspension expedient, is it credible that this *happy* feature would be blotted out forever, and the power given to the Executive to determine "when the public safety may require" the suspension?

Whether they *did* that or not will now be considered.

Without the adoption of this clause the Federal Government would or would not have had the power to suspend the privilege of the Writ. Let it be assumed (what is not admitted, however) that it *would*. It is clear nevertheless that the *Judiciary* could not have had it, for even now their authority to issue that Writ is given, not by the Constitution, but by the *Legislature*. Nor could the *President* have had it, for his claim to that power is rested solely on the existence of this section; (indeed, if the power has been given to him under any other clause, it weakens, if it does not entirely negative, the presumption that it is given to him by the 9th section;) as, then, this power could not belong to the *Judiciary*, or to the *President*, it follows that it would belong to the *Legislature*. On the other hand, let it be assumed that it is this section which gives that *power* to the Federal Government, yet the like reasoning will show that it can only be exercised by the *Legislature*. Thus as it was by concession a power which could only have been exercised by the *Parliament* in England, or by the *Legislatures* of the several States, those who now attribute it to the President must show that that section contains three things—

1st. The grant of the *power*. 2d. That those who granted it, *changed* it from the Legislative department in which, under the English and American Constitutions, it always had been, and but for this specific change would have remained, to the President, or *Executive* department of the Government; and 3d. That this power to suspend, is a *limited* one.

B

Now two of those things may be found in that section. 1st, the *grant* of the *power*, and 2d, *a limit* to the power thus granted, but that is all; the 3d is not declared, there is not in the whole instrument the gleam of an intention to change the old, accustomed and only organ of this power. It has been admitted that "the Constitution does not expressly say by what department of the Government this privilege is to be denied or deferred." But it is clear that a grant of the *power*, with a *limit* to it does no more change and make the *President* the organ which is to exercise it, than would the mere admission that the power existed without the grant, make *him* that organ.

Whether then the *power* to suspend existed without, or is given by, that section, it does not change the organ which had theretofore exercised it. But as a general power to suspend, whether assumed to exist without, or given only by, that section, would have enabled Congress to suspend that privilege at any time and for any cause, or even without a cause; and as the people of the United States "regarded that as a very exceptional fact, and wholly inadmissible by them," they meant not to exclude congressional law, as some would have it inferred, but to limit congressional *power ;* and that they did by prescribing the conditions on which alone Congress should ever exercise the power. In other words, they did not change the trusteeship of this, their privilege, but they did very greatly limit the *power* of their trustees.

Those who argue for the President's suspending power, feel themselves sorely pressed by the analogy of the English law, and the better to get rid of it they insist that suspending the privilege of the Writ, is not an English law expression; that the word *suspended*, as applied to the *privilege*, is not a word of the common law, or of any other system of laws in particular. That the phrase, the *privilege* of the Writ of Habeas Corpus shall not be *suspended*, was *first* introduced into the *Constitution* of the *United States*, and *therefore*, we should not look to English constitutional history or law for the meaning of those words, or for an argument from analogy. It would be quite as pertinent to tell us to study Theology without the Bible, or American Literature without Chaucer, Shakespeare, or Milton, or our own language without an English Dictionary, as to require us to study, or even understand that part of our own Constitution, without a knowledge of the *privileges* of Englishmen, and of the great charters and statutes in which they are recorded.

The American colonists always claimed to possess, and the Continental Congress of 1774 declared they were entitled to, all the rights, liberties, and immunities of free and natural born subjects within the realm of England.—Hurd. p. 105.

" The colonists," said Chatham, "are equally entitled with yourselves to all the natural rights of mankind, and the peculiar *privileges* of Englishmen."

The colonists were devoted to liberty, but it was to the principles of *English* liberty. These principles were incorporated into their minds, " from their extraction, their religion, the works they read, and the form of their colonial governments"—(Smythe's Lectures, 593,) the latter of which were modeled on that of England. In 1774, Mr. Burke said of the colonies, " In no country in the world is the law so general a study. * * No books save those of devotion are so generally sent from England thither than on law. I hear they have sold nearly as many of Blackstone's Commentaries in America as in England." In October, 1768, the Massachusetts Assembly resolved, "That all the essential rights, liberties, *privileges*, and immunities of the people of Great Britain had been fully confirmed to them by Magna Charta, and by former and latter Acts of Parliament, and in a petition from the· New York Convention to the House of Commons, they said, " It is from and under the English Constitution we derive all our civil and religious rights and liberties." And Mr. Burke said, "English *privileges* have made America all that it is; and English privileges, alone, will make it all it can be."

Of a people, who risked a revolution to secure for themselves and their posterity the great principles of English liberty, we could readily infer, what indeed we know, that they would be guided by the same principles in organizing a government for themselves, and it necessarily follows that they would use words and phrases like those in which they had been accustomed to find these principles recorded. It will be found, therefore, that those words in the Constitution were well known to, and were used by, writers on the Common Law and by statesmen; and that they were not singly or together first used in the Constitution of the United States. Before noticing the meaning and application given to them, and the arguments based on both, by those who assign the suspending power to the President—the following remarks are submitted:

Privilege.—In its legal and political acceptation in England and in the American colonies, this word does not signify what it may have originally meant, viz., a peculiar benefit or immunity which one citizen enjoyed beyond that of other citizens; but the word *privilege* was in common use, to signify those civil and political *rights* claimed by Englishmen as peculiar to them and not common to other nations. In commenting on the words of the 29th chap. of Magna Charta, 9 Hen. 3. "Nullus liber homo capiatur, vel imprisonetur, aut dissaisietur de aliquo libero tenemento suo, vel *libertatibus* vel liberis consuetudinibus, &c.—Professor Sullivan says, "The word '*libertatibus*' comprehends,—1. The *Laws of the realm* that every man should freely enjoy such advantages and *privileges* as those laws give him.—2. It signifies the privileges that *some* of the subjects, whether single persons or bodies corporate, have above others, by the lawful grant of the King.—Lec. 41, p. 372.

In the act of 31 Charles I. chap. 10, sec. 2, which abolished the court of Star Chamber, it is declared that the council table "had lately ventured to determine of the liberty of the subject contrary to the laws of the land, and the rights and *privileges* of the people."

In the Parliament that assembled in 1640, Waller denounced certain divines as manifestly in the wrong in that which concerns the liberties and *privileges* of the subjects of England.

In the speech made by George I. on the introduction of the Peerage Bill by the Ministers, he said, "As the civil rights and *privileges* of my subjects claim my concern," &c., and in his speech dissolving Parliament, in 1734, he said, "The happiness of my people depends upon my preserving to them all their legal rights and *privileges,* as established under the present settlement of the crown," &c.

In a remonstrance drawn by Otis, in 1761, for the Massachusetts Assembly, an act of the Governor and Council was denounced as "an invasion of the most darling *privilege,* the right of originating all taxes."—4 Grah., 87.

In 1745, Virginia resolved that the most substantial and distinguished part of their political birth-right was the *privilege* of being taxed exclusively by themselves, and that they had always exercised this privilege.—4 Grah., 203.

The Convention of the Colonies, which met in New York in 1765, voted that the most essential of their liberties were the *privileges* of taxing themselves and of trial by jury.—4 Gra., 217. These and the like words, in almost every page of English and American history, show the sense in which the word *privilege* was used. But the framers of the Constitution used the same word in article 4, section 2, of the Constitution. "The citizens of each State shall be entitled to all *privileges* and immunities of citizens in the several States;" and it is fortunate that these words, and the word *privilege* used in the *Habeas Corpus* clause, have been explained by a Judge, of the tone or ring of whose opinion no one can complain.

In the case of *Corfield* v. *Coryell*, 4 Wash. C. C. Rep. 380, Judge Washington said, "The inquiry is, what are the *privileges* and immunities of citizens of the several States? We feel no hesitation in confining these expressions to those *privileges* and immunities which are in their nature *fundamental;* which belong of *right* to the citizens of all free Governments. * * They may all be comprehended under the following general heads: The enjoyment of life and liberty, and to pursue and obtain happiness and safety; subject, nevertheless, to such restraints as the Government may justly prescribe for the general good of the whole. The *right* of a citizen of one State to pass through, or to reside in any other State, for purposes of trade, &c., *to claim the benefit of the Writ of Habeas Corpus*, &c., may be mentioned as some of the particular *privileges* and immunities of citizens, which are clearly embraced by the general description of *privileges*, which are deemed to be fundamental, to which may be added the elective franchise," &c.

This, then, is the meaning of the word *privilege* and the sense in which it is to be read in the Habeas Corpus clause, viz: "The *right* to claim the benefit of the *Writ of Habeas Corpus* shall not be *suspended*," &c. The privilege of a thing then means the *right* to a thing; and the privilege of the Writ of Habeas Corpus, means the right to the Writ of Habeas Corpus, just as the phrase, the *privilege of trial by jury*, means the right to trial by jury. The idea of the former is, too, quite as old as the latter. Nor is the phrase itself, viz: "The *privilege of the Writ of Habeas Corpus*," a new one. It was known and used in England nearly one hundred years before our Constitution was made. In 1692, the Province of Massachusetts was organized under a new charter, under which the General Court passed certain laws, one of them claiming the *benefit* of the Writ of Habeas Corpus was rejected (by the King) on the ground that "the *privilege* had not yet been granted to the plantations."—1 Barry's Hist. Mass. This colonial act adopted, it is said, the Habeas Corpus Act of 31, Charles II., and it was disallowed in 1695.—Hurd on Hab. Corp., p. 111. But "the *right* to the Writ, was, before that time claimed as one of the existing *privileges* of the Colonists in Massachusetts," Hurd, p. 110, and in a book, the second edition of which was published in England in the year 1767, named like, and based upon Henry Care's British Liberties, it is said:—

"Many gentlemen that refused (to grant supplies to Charles the First) were imprisoned or sent abroad by the King and his privy council, and the Judges refused, to several that applied for it, the *privilege of the Writ of Habeas Corpus*, to which they were entitled by the ancient common law of the realm." That, be it observed, was before the Petition of Right or the passage of the Habeas Corpus Act.

Not only then was it known that the word privilege signified the *right* to the Writ of Habeas Corpus, as it did to the trial by jury, and other rights of the people of England, but the phrase, "the PRIVILEGE of the Writ of Habeas Corpus," appears to have been well known to and used in the Colonies and in England, at least as early as 1692; and, it may be here stated, that the whole clause now in the Constitution of the United States, *including* the word *suspended*, as applied to the *privilege*, was borrowed from the Constitution of Massachusetts, in which it had been used ten years before; and not only that, but the *privilege* had actually been *suspended* by the Legislature of Massachusetts a year before the Constitution of the United States was adopted.

In September, 1778, a State Convention was called in Massachusetts. They framed a Constitution, which, having been approved by the people, the Convention adopted in June, 1780. The city of Boston agreed to it, "but with proposed alterations, one of them respecting the privilege of the Writ of Habeas Corpus; with regard to this, they wished that the privilege should be more accurately defined and more liberally granted, so that citizens should not be subject to confinement for *suspicion*."—Barry's Hist. Mass.. vol. 3, p. 177–8. The article itself is in the following words:— "Chap. 9, Art. 7. The *privilege* and benefit of the Writ of *Habeas Corpus* shall be enjoyed in this Commonwealth in the most free, easy, cheap, expeditious, and ample manner; and shall not be *suspended* by the Legislature except upon the most urgent and pressing occasion, and for a limited time, not exceeding twelve months." A reference to the Habeas Corpus clause offered by Mr. Pinckney, on August 20th, and hereinbefore copied, will show that it was taken, word for word, (except, indeed, the "free. easy, and cheap," words,) from the Constitution of Massachusetts; and the whole argument based on the want of analogy between the English Constitution and our own, is now cut up, root and branch, by, not the analogy, but the identity between this legislative suspending clause of Massachusetts and that in the Constitution of the United States. If it was not a loose, it was surely then an "inaccurate expression," to say that those words "were *first* introduced into the Constitution of the United States."

The occasion of the suspension was Shay's Rebellion—after which, viz: (on Nov. 10, 1786,) the privilege of the writ was suspended for eight months.—Barry's Hist. vol. 3, p. 235.

It is not then correct to say that the expression "suspending the privilege" was first introduced into the Constitution of the United States. Nor, indeed, was the thing itself, or the like expressions unknown here or in England.

To *suspend* signifies to withhold, "to debar" for a time, from the execution of an office or the enjoyment of a revenue or of any *privilege*.— *Worcester*. To debar from any privilege, to cause to cease for a time from operation or effect, as to suspend the Habeas Corpus Act. Suspended, prevented from enjoying a right.— *Webster*. That the privilege of the Writ of Habeas Corpus shall not be suspended, means then, that the right to the Writ shall not cease for a time, unless, &c.

1. It is very obvious, therefore, why the word *privilege* was made the subject of the predicate *suspended.*

In relation to the Government of the United States, there was no Habeas Corpus *Act;* for while the Writ was, the Habeas Corpus *Acts* were not, the same in the several States; nor could it be known whether Congress would ever pass such an Act, (which, indeed, they have not yet passed;) consequently there was no Act, present or future, to be suspended.

2. Nor, had they suspended the Act of 31 Chas. II., or any other act, would that have effected their object; because as the Common Law privilege of, or right to, the Writ was not given by an Act, the suspension or even the repeal of the Act would have left the privilege or *right* unaffected.—See Hur. Hab. Cor., p. 133.

3. It would not have been logical to have said that the *Writ* should not be suspended, because that would have been to suspend a remedy while leaving the privilege of, or right to, the Writ untouched, and it would possibly have left the privilege, or right itself, open to be suspended at any time; for it might have been contended that the suspending power was only prohibited from suspending the *Writ,* but was not prohibited from suspending the privilege or right itself before invasion or rebellion; it follows, therefore, that the Convention was logically obliged to say that the *privilege* should not be suspended: thus forever guarding the right itself, save only in the cases mentioned in the clause. Nor could any word but *suspended* have been used. For the right to the writ being an original and inherent right—it could only have been suspended; it could not have been taken away entirely. Nor was the suspending a privilege or right a novelty in English law. The suspending power had long been a subject of legal and parliamentary discussion in England. The power itself, or the expediency of exercising it, had never been denied to parliament, but when it was claimed and exercised for and by the King, as the like power is now claimed for the President, the people by the Declaration and Bill of Rights declared and ordained that by the Common Law it never had and that it never should be exercised by their Executive, but by their Legislature only.

In speaking on Fox's East India Bill, Mr. Burke said, "The rights of men, that is to say the natural rights of mankind, are, indeed, sacred things. If these natural rights are further secured against power and authority by written instruments and positive engagements, they are in a little better condition. Indeed, this formal recognition by the sovereign power, of an original right in the subject, can never be subverted but by rooting up the radical principles of government, and even of society itself. The charters which we call by distinction *Great* are public instruments of this nature, I mean the charters of King John and King Henry III., and the rights secured by these instruments may, without any deceitful ambiguity, be very fairly called the Chartered Rights of Men.

" But, sir, the East India Charter is a charter to establish monopoly, and to create power." " These chartered rights (viz., of the East India Company) do at least *suspend* the natural *rights* of mankind at large, and in their very frame and constitution are liable to fall into a direct violation of them." The *privilege* of the writ of Habeas Corpus is one of the natural privileges secured to men by the Great Charters. Mr. Burke included it among the others, so that to speak of *suspending* that privilege was not then a novelty to the lawyers or statesmen of England. And why should it have been one to the lawyers and statesmen of the United States ? In fact they well knew, and had before complained of the suspension of a like privilege.

The right of the people to legislate for themselves being a natural right, and by law as much a privilege as any other belonging to Englishmen, the King, in Parliament, was justly complained of for *suspending* our own legislatures, " and also for suspending the operation of laws." It has been asserted " that the Habeas Corpus *Act* of 31 Charles II. has never been suspended for a moment ;" and that the English Imprisonment Acts used no such *words* as to the English Habeas Corpus Statute or Writ, and hence it is left to be inferred that the use of the word *suspended* in the Constitution was unknown to the English law. (That argument would not have been used as a make-weight had it not been for the impression of the writer that the expression had been first used in the Constitution of the United States ; that has been shown to be incorrect, but still the assertion may be noticed, as it involves an argument against, and not for, the President's power.) It may be literally true that the Habeas Corpus *Act* has never been suspended. Lord Brougham had before made the same remark.—Pol. Philos., vol. 3. But. in the sense in which Blackstone and other legal writers used the expression, it is either true, or it is clear that during more than a century the *privilege* of the writ of Habeas Corpus has been from time to time *suspended* even in England. The dilemma is unavoidable.

Blackstone's Commentaries were first published in 1765–8. But in the book before mentioned, entitled "English Liberties," &c., and written before that, it is said: "If the Legislature leaves the Executive power in possession of a right to imprison those subjects, who can give security for their good behaviour—there is an end of liberty: unless they are taken up in order to answer, without delay, for a capital crime; in which case they are really free. The *Habeas Corpus Act* was intended to render the subject safe in this particular. Why a *suspension* of it hath ever been permitted, politicians best can answer. * * James II., when Monmouth was in actual rebellion against him, did not demand it. * * *Montesquieu* knew an English Parliament had more than once permitted a temporary *suspension* of the *Habeas Corpus Act*."—Introduction, pp. 21–22.

"This Act (31 Charles II.) has been at various times *suspended*, with respect to the power of imprisonment vested in the Crown, upon occasions of public alarm; such *suspension* usually being for a very short period. The general title given to such temporary acts has been, 'An Act to empower his Majesty to secure and detain such persons as his Majesty shall *suspect* are conspiring against his person and Government. The following are acts of that description: 1 W. & M., St. 1, ch. 7, 19; 7 and 8 W., 3, ch. 11; 6 Anne, ch. 15; 7 Anne, ch. 9; 1 Geo. I., ch. 8, 30; 17 Geo. II., ch. 6; 19 Geo. II., ch. 1; 17 Geo. III., ch. 9; 34 Geo. III., ch. 54, (May 23, 1794,) followed by several acts during the war then existing."—*Evans' Note:* cited in Chitty's Statutes, vol. 1, p. 344.

The 17 Geo. III., ch. 9, was an Act introduced in 1777 to enable the King, "any law or statute to the contrary notwithstanding," to detain in prison all who were charged with, or suspected of, committing treason in America or on the high seas, or of being guilty of what the Government denominated piracy. "This was another of those unhappy measures which it had so long been the policy of the King and his Ministers to recommend. and which sought to make war in the Colonies, not so much by the thunder of artillery, as by the *brutum fulmen* of Parliament." "It was a practical *suspension* of the *Habeas Corpus Act*. It called men pirates, who, at the blackest could only be looked upon as rebels, and thus, by a strained interpretation of the common law, sought to debase morally, the criminality of acts for which the legal penalty remained the same." The Marquis of Rockingham, Fox, Dunning, and their friends all denounced it as a suspension of the Habeas Corpus Act.—McKnight's Life of Burke, vol. 2, p. 163–164. The Act of 34 George III., chap. 54, was avowed by the Minister, Pitt, to be a *partial suspension* of the Habeas Corpus Act; and as such it was defended by Adair and denounced by Fox and Sheridan.—Annals of Great Britain, vol. 3, p. 22 and 24. " In 1817 the measures proposed by the Minister, (and which passed,) were the temporary *suspension* of the Habeas Corpus Act."—Bissett's England, vol. 3, p. 341. "An Act was passed for the continuing until the 1st of March, 1818, the suspension of the Habeas Corpus Act."—Bissett, vol. 3, p. 341.

" The salutary effects of the *suspension* of the Habeas Corpus Act in the year 1817."—Allison's Europe, vol. 1, chap. 4, p. 23. It was suspended in Ireland in 1822.—1 Allison, chap. 10, p. 123. and again in 1848.—4 Allison, chap. 43, p. 138. Chap. 56, p. 52. And Allison, be it remembered, is a lawyer as well as a historian. John Stuart Mill, in Frazer's Magazine for February, 1862, speaks of England having "*suspended* the Habeas Corpus Act."

In 8 Mod. Rep., p. 96, there are reported the cases of the King vs. the Earl of Orrery, and five others, who, being committed by the Secretary of State for high treason, moved for leave to enter their prayer under the Habeas Corpus Act of 31 Car. 2. The report says: " This (Habeas Corpus) Act was now by another act of George I., chap. 1, sec. 1, *suspended* for a time." Neither the counsel for the prisoner nor for the King questioned but that the Act had been suspended. They both used the word *suspended*, and Ailsbury's case was cited.

The case of Lord Ailsbury there referred to is that of Rex vs. the Earl of Ailsbury.—Comberbach's Rep. 421, and reported also in Cases Tempore Holt, p. 84.—In Hil. Term., 9, William III. Lord Ailsbury prayed to be bailed, having entered his prayer the first week of this term.   He was committed in March last, but (the report proceeds) " the Habeas Corpus Act was *suspended*, by a late statute, till September, and by a later statute until December, so that he could not come sooner to enter his prayer, and per Cur., Holt, Ch. J., " when the power of the Court was taken away from bailing, if he doth not make his prayer the first term, when the law is open, he cannot do it afterwards upon the Habeas Corpus Act : but when the *Act* is *suspended* it must be understood that he must do it the first term after the *suspension*.   And so we held upon the former *Act* of *suspension*."

It may be that from the time of Lord Chief Justice Holt, to John Stuart Mill, in 1862, Chief Justices, Judges, lawyers, and writers upon law, statesmen, and historians, have spoken loosely on this point.   But what did they mean—and suppose they would be understood by others to mean ?   During the existence of those suspending acts, it is true that *some* people were entitled to the privilege of the Habeas Corpus Act; therefore, *as to them*, the Act was not suspended, and so, to speak literally, the *Act*, as a whole, and as applying to *all* persons, was not suspended.   But as the Habeas Corpus Act might be suspended, as readily as repealed, as to all persons, why, then, could it not be suspended as to some of them? There is no technical impossibility in such a suspension, and it was just that suspension, and that only, which Blackstone, and all who have so termed it, meant.   One citation will show that.

" In cases of conspiracy or meditated treason against the King, it is not unusual to vest a power in the King of apprehending and detaining suspected persons, without bail or main prize, which, *as to them*, operates as a *suspension* of the Habeas Corpus Act."— Jacob's Law, Dict. Title Government.   And that, too, was Mr. Madison's opinion as to the suspension of the privilege under our Constitution.—Rep. on Virg. Res.

But either the *Act* has been suspended, or the *privilege* has been suspended.   The dilemma is unavoidable.   Thus the suspending acts must have done one of four things, as it respected the persons to whom it was meant to apply them, viz: 1. To *repeal* the Habeas Corpus Act; or, 2d, to *suspend* the Act; or, 3d, to *suspend* the

Writ; or, 4th, to suspend the *privilege* of, or right to, the *Writ* or *Act*. Those who say that they did not even *suspend* the Act, cannot say that they *repealed* it as to any body; nor, as they insist, did they suspend it; and, for a still stronger reason, they did not suspend the *Writ;* it follows, therefore, that it must have been the *privilege* itself which they *suspended*. No matter that the acts did not use the word *privilege;* they did in legal intendment and effect declare, that certain persons should not, for a limited time, have a *right* to apply for the Writ of Habeas Corpus, and when the Courts refused them the *Writ*, they did such persons no wrong; for that there cannot be any wrong, denial, or delay, when there is no right, is a maxim both of the civil and common law.

What has thus been said, may now be applied in answer to the main positions in favor of the President's suspending power; and the first is, that the privilege mentioned in the clause is the privilege of an *imprisoned* or detained person, of being bailed, &c., &c. That "the warrant of arrest *with* the *order* that the party's privilege be *denied* for a season, *is suspension.*" That "the power to imprison *and* to *deny* or *delay* a discharge from imprisonment, is an Executive power; therefore the suspension is an Executive power. Is it, however, true that there is no privilege in the Constitutional sense of the word, before a person has been arrested? When, in 1692, the people of Massachusetts passed a Habeas Corpus Act, and the King refused to approve it, because, as he said, "the *privilege* had not been *granted* to the plantations," did he mean to say that that privilege did not exist because they had not all been ARRESTED? If the status of imprisonment be essential to the existence of the *privilege* of the Writ, it was very fortunate for the people of Massachusetts that the King had not granted to them *that* privilege. When the people of England have, from age to age, clamored for their privileges, and that they should be secured to them by charter upon charter, did they ever suppose that their own *imprisonment* was an element, and an essential one, of their chartered *privileges?* Have not the people the privilege of trial by jury without being in Court as parties, plaintiff, or defendant? Surely, the privilege of, or right to, a thing, is essentially different from the enjoyment of that right. That a man cannot exercise his privilege of, or right to demand, the Writ of Habeas Corpus, till he has been imprisoned, is true; but the imprisonment is not the privilege, or any element of it, it but gives occasion for the exercise of it. The privilege does not then "*subsist* in *remedy*." But it is further objected, that "it is *impossible* to suppose that, in speaking of suspending the privilege of the Writ, it (the Constitution) meant by one act of *law*, as if it had spoken of the *Writ* alone, or of the Habeas Corpus *Act*." That sentence was penned by a gentleman who then overlooked the fact, that the Constitution of Massachusetts, made seven years before that of the United States, contained precisely the same clause. That it *did* mean just what that writer says it was IMPOSSIBLE it *could* mean, viz: that the privilege should be suspended by *one act* of *law;* and he overlooked the further fact, that instead of it being impossible to suspend the privilege by *one* act of *law*, that impossibility had actually been performed by the Legislature of Massachusetts one year before the Constitution of the United States was made; and that that impossible act, was well known to every member of the Federal Convention.

Besides, to affirm that the power to deny the privilege is an Executive power begs the question ; and that it is *not* an Executive function is thus proved. If the Constitution had declared that " the privilege of the Writ of Habeas Corpus may be suspended at *any time*," the power must have been exercised by the same department which ought now to exercise it ; for the present limitation of time does but limit the *power* without changing the *organ* of that power. But that absolute power to suspend the privilege would have been but a parliamentary power, and the case would *then* have been analogous to, and even identical with, parliamentary law ; and as such a power had always been in the Legislature of England, and in the Legislatures of the respective States and *not* in their respective *Executives*, so it would have belonged to the *Legislature* of the United States, and *not* to their Executive by virtue of his office. Now the words in the existing clause only require the *same organ* to limit its power to *specified* occasions, instead of exercising it on *any* occasion ; so that the limited power *remains* with the organ of the greater power, viz., with the Legislature ; therefore the power to deny the privilege does *not* belong to the Executive by virtue of his office. Again, an arrest (according to law) is an Executive act, and generally does, and always can happen without an order to suspend the privilege of the party arrested; if then, by the one act of the Executive the party has been arrested, but *without* an order denying his privilege, the latter has not been suspended; but can it not *afterwards* (and during his detention) be suspended? To deny that would be absurd; but that subsequent act of *denial* cannot be the act of arrest or any part of it, hence the *order* of denial *alone* must be the act of suspension, which, therefore, is not the warrant of arrest *with* the order, &c.; and as the act which thus suspends the privilege has no connection with the act of arrest, it is not essential that it should proceed from the same actor, and as "a single order (of the legislature,) founded on the authority of the Constitution," would be as effective a suspension as a single order (of the President,) founded on the same authority, therefore, an act of the Legislature, viz., a *legislative order*, "is all that is necessary to suspend the privilege," and consequently, it "*is suspension under the Constitution.*"

III. It has been insisted also,—1, That "all the conditions of the exercise of the power described in the Habeas Corpus clause, are of Executive cognizance; that is to say, rebellion or invasion *and* the *requirement of the public safety* in the times of either," and 2, That the power to suspend the privilege of the Writ "is *inseparably* connected with rebellion or invasion."

"It is the duty of the office, in both its civil and military aspects, to suppress insurrections and repel invasions." "That no legislative act is necessary or proper to give cognizance of these facts to the Executive department;" that, unlike Parliament, which is the highest power in England and gives the authority, our Constitution is higher than Congress, and "is itself the *authority*, and *all* that remains is to execute it." The answers to these are—1, one. and the most essential, of the conditions, viz., ("when the public safety may require it,") is *not* of Executive, but is of Legislative cognizance.—2, that to suspend the *right* of a citizen is not the duty of the Executive in its civil or its military aspect.

When, in 1777, a bill was introduced into the English Parliament to suspend the privilege of the Writ of Habeas Corpus as to Americans engaged, or suspected of being engaged, in the rebellion,

Mr. Fox and his friends opposed the bill, and "they succeeded in modifying some of its most arbitrary features."—McKnight's Life of Burke; vol. 2, p. 164. Is it of less consequence to American citizens, that *they* should have the like protection? Or that their immediate representatives shall have the right to judge whether the public safety does actually require the suspension of their privilege? or at least to modify the proceeding as was done in England?

Rebellion and invasion are great physical facts, which all can see, and about which there can be but one judgment. These the Executive may readily know, but the Constitution does not authorize the privilege of the Habeas Corpus to be suspended upon either rebellion or invasion. Granting that they exist, nevertheless the Constitution expressly declares that "The privilege shall *not* be suspended *unless* when the PUBLIC SAFETY may require it." Is it true, then, that no Legislative act is necessary or *proper* to give cognizance of *that* fact to the Executive? There is not, among the innumerable subjects of Legislative cognizance, one so essentially of that class as the requirement of *public safety*. What it may or may not require depends on expediency and sound public policy; and the requirement itself is essentially the judgment which the competent authority shall pronounce on the field of events, which does in their judgment influence the safety of the public. Let there be rebellion or invasion, but what new rules of conduct shall be prescribed on their account? If new laws be required, Congress alone can make them. If property is to be taken, Congress alone can take it. Shall then the privilege of privileges—shall liberty itself be subjected to a department, incapable of making any law, or of prescribing a rule of conduct for anybody? Laws are but means to guard the liberty of the citizen, and to the Legislature alone have the people intrusted the power of making and modifying the laws; have they then given to the Executive power to take away liberty itself?—the very end for which the law was made.

Granted that the public safety may require its suspension, shall the President only, or shall Congress, say how long that safety requires it, and when it shall cease? or which of them shall say in what places, or upon what persons, or on what conditions only, the suspension shall operate? If it shall be notorious that warrants of arrest have been left in blank, with power in corrupt and arbitrary Secretaries to fill them up, as they shall find a victim, shall the President be permitted to depute that discretionary power to such officers, to be exercised when, where, and upon whom they shall think fit? It may be replied that this might follow even if the Legislature had suspended the privilege, for then the imprisonment would still be the sole act of the President. But the answers are: 1. Power held under the will of another is never so much abused, and can never be so dangerous as when it is not so held; hence, the President and his dependents would be less likely to abuse it when held by the sufferance of Congress only, than if it were held under the Constitution, and above Congress. 2. A power given by Congress could be given upon *terms*, in case of abuse they could require an account of it, its rightful possessors could call the public attention to its abuse, it would, in short, have every check and safeguard which are possible to be given to it; but if the Constitution has given the power to the Executive, the Congress cannot require an account of its use, or take it away in case of its abuse. They themselves may be among its victims.

But does it belong to his office in its *civil* aspect? Hamilton has said that "the essence of legislative authority is to *enact* laws, or in other words, to *prescribe* rules for the regulation of the society; while the *execution* of the laws, and the employment of the common strength, either for this purpose, or for the common defense, seems to comprise *all* the functions of the Executive Magistrate.—" Fed. No. 75. And Mr. Madison said :—Report on Virg. Res.—" It has become an axiom in the science of government, that a separation of the legislative and executive departments, is necessary to the preservation of public *liberty*. Nowhere has this axiom been better understood in theory, or more carefully pursued in practice, than in the United States."

The duty, then, of the Executive office is to take care that the laws shall be executed, and that presupposes the existence of the laws to be executed. But those laws bind the President as well as any private citizen; they say to him—The law allows, nay, enjoins upon you, to arrest whosoever shall violate the law, but it next enjoins the Judge to hear that accusation, and to decide between the Executive and the accused, and to bail, remand, or try him accord-

c

ing to law; so that if, by the laws of the land, he has deserved to be punished, "then by the same laws also he may, and by no other he ought, to be judged, and acquitted, or condemned." If then " the warrant of arrest, with the order that the party's privilege be denied for a season, is suspension," what is that *order* but a *law*, and the power to make it, but power to *make a law?* The law had given the privilege, this order takes it away; the law had said the prisoner ought to be heard, and bailed, released, or tried by a Judge; this order prohibits the Judge from bailing, or releasing, or trying; even the prisoner himself need not be informed of the accusation against him. What is this but to make a law abrogating, for a season, all laws, which, from Magna Charta to the Constitution, have solemnly declared that "no freeman shall be taken, or imprisoned, or passed upon but by the law of the land" —that is by judicial proceedings? The President considers, in his own mind, what the public safety requires, and, thereupon, he *legislates*—he wills the law for each prisoner. In the language of Mr. Jefferson, he is " himself the accuser, counsel, judge and jury; whose suspicion may be the evidence, his *order* the sentence, his officer the jailor, and his breast the sole record of the transaction." It is incredible that such is the duty of the office in its *civil* aspect.

3. Is it so in its military aspect? " Congress (not the President) shall have power to declare war, raise and support armies, to provide for calling forth the militia to execute the laws of the Union, suppress insurrection, and repel invasion."—Const. Art 1, sec. 8.

Be it remembered that this power is claimed to have been given to the President alone. If that, or any other power within the Constitutional grant be necessary in case of rebellion or invasion, Congress will judge of the requirements of the public safety, and upon their own motion, or on demand of the Executive, may give him the power of the whole government. The Legislature is here, and in all free governments, the organ of the national will. The Executive but enforces that will. He upholds and enforces the rights of the people, he cannot suspend or take their rights away. If the law has been violated, then by, and according to, the same law, he takes care that the violators are arrested; there his duty ceases; for the Judges alone, who are equal in authority with himself, can pass upon or judge the alleged violator of it ; but if the President himself passes upon him, or withholds him from their judgment, *he* then becomes the violator of the law, he usurps the functions of the Judiciary, and he is not in the performance of his office.

This becomes evident from a view of the whole spirit, and even the letter, of the Federal, and the several State Constitutions.

To suspend the privilege of the Writ of Habeas Corpus, is to suspend the laws and the *execution* of the laws ; and as that power is by express words in some, and by the fair intendment and effect of all the State Constitutions, prohibited to the Executive, and when suffered at all, is confined to the Legislature, both by the Constitutions made *before* as well as since that of the United States, it is the highest evidence, that the same people did not mean to give, and that in their opinion they did not give, that power to the Federal Executive, but limited it to the Legislature. 1. It *suspends* the laws, it suspends the right itself. It suspends every law from and since Magna Charta, which secures the right. It suspends the Bill of Rights in every State which has such a bill, and few are without one. It suspends that part of the Constitution of every State made before as well as since the Federal Constitution, which ordains, and they all ordain, that the privilege of the Writ of Habeas Corpus shall not be suspended, save by the Legislature.

By section 12 of the Bill of Rights in the Constitution of Pennsylvania, it is ordained that *"No power of suspending law shall be exercised, unless by the Legislature or its authority."* The like provision, with the addition, generally, that the execution of the laws shall not be suspended, was ordained before the adoption of the Constitution of the United States, in the Bills of Rights or Constitutions of Massachusetts, New York, Virginia, North Carolina, Maryland ; and since that time in the Bills of Rights or Constitution of New Hampshire, Vermont, Connecticut, New Jersey, Georgia, Kentucky, Rhode Island, Tennessee, Ohio, Indiana, Mississippi, Maine, and Alabama, and it may be in others ; and in not a single instance is that power given, even by implication, to the Executive.

But it suspends the *execution* of the laws ; a thing as much forbidden by the intent, and as often by the words of those Bills of

Rights and Constitutions, as that of suspending the laws themselves. The power which suspends the privilege, does in effect suspend the execution of every law which enjoins judges to issue, and officers to execute, the Writ of Habeas Corpus. From the moment that the executive *fiat* goes forth, the arm of the Judiciary is arrested, and those laws can no longer be executed.

In still further evidence that the power of suspension was not meant to be taken from the Legislature and given to the President, it appears that in every State Constitution in which the Habeas Corpus is mentioned, (and it is mentioned in perhaps every one of them, in terms like, or identical with, that of the United States,) the power is conferred only upon the Legislature; in no instance is it given to the Executive; and in the amended Constitution of Virginia it is taken from both.

In the Federal Convention, on June 4th, Mr. Gerry moved that " the National Executive shall have a right to negative any legislative act which shall not be afterwards passed, unless by——parts of each branch," &c. It was moved to amend so as to read, " Resolved that the National Executive have a power to SUSPEND any legislative act for ——," and the amendment was *unanimously negatived*. That was the only attempt ever made in the Federal Convention to give to the Executive a suspending power.

The position of the Clause.—It has been said that " the present position of the clause in the Constitution is not of the least consequence; according to the Journal of the Convention, the clause was offered as an amendment to the fourth section of the article on the Judiciary. If position in a section of an article carries power to the article, then the original motion as adopted carried power to the Judiciary, and must have regarded suspension of the privilege as a judicial act, and *not* as dependant on a *legislative* act." It is submitted that that is a *non sequitur*.

1. A reference to the history hereinbefore given of the Judiciary clause which is *now* clause 3, Sec. II., Art. III.; will show that it limited the *place* where trials in criminal cases should be had to the State in which they should be committed—that was a limitation upon the power of Congress, without which they might have enacted that the trial should be elsewhere; and the latter sentence of the section, viz., "as to crimes not committed within any State, the trial

shall be at such place or places as *Congress* may by law *have* directed," is also restrictive, because it prohibits a trial at any place other than where Congress shall *have* directed, viz., before the commission of the specific offence; so that the whole subject of the section was a restriction upon the power of *Congress*, and when Mr. Morris offered the Habeas Corpus clause as an amendment to it, it shows, when read in connection with it, that it also, was (for greater caution) a limitation upon the power of *Congress*.

It has been further objected: " In *opposition* to an intention to leave the power to *Congress*, observe the striking departure from parallel of the *second* clause of Section 9, Article I., from the *first* clause of the same section :

"*First* Clause.—'The migration or importation of such persons, &c., shall not be prohibited by Congress before the year 1808, but a tax or duty (expressly within the power of Congress, section 8) may be imposed on such importation.'

"*Second* Clause.—'The privilege of the Writ, &c., shall not be suspended, unless when, &c., the public safety may require it,' and the word 'Legislature' dropped from Mr. Pinckney's clause."

The answer to " the departure from parallel" is this :—Had the word " Congress" been omitted from the first clause, so as to read " the importation, &c., shall not be prohibited," &c., that might have been construed as prohibiting not only Congress but the States from abolishing the slave trade before the year 1808, but the insertion of the word " Congress," prohibited them only, and thus "in the interim all the States were at liberty to prohibit it."—Mass. Debates, p. 117. And the limitation on taxing was inserted, lest a prohibitory tax should be imposed by Congress, (see Virg. Deb., p. 322–324,) so the parallel is not departed from.

Passing from the Convention which prepared, to the State Conventions which ratified and made it, what was their opinion of the clause ?

So soon as the Federal Constitution had been framed, it was submitted to Conventions of the respective States. The members of those Conventions were generally the ablest in the States, and among them were the chief men who had themselves framed the Constitution, and who, of course, knew what its several clauses meant.

In the New York Convention there were, among others, Hamilton, Jay, Morris, and the Livingstons. In that of Massachusetts, were Adams, Hancock, Cushing, and Gorham. In that of Virginia, were Madison, Mason, Randolph, and Henry. It has been observed, that in the Federal Convention, this *Habeas Corpus* clause was adopted with very little debate. That is true, also, of the State Conventions; for example, in that of New York, it is recorded that "the Committee (of the Whole) then proceeded through sections 8, *nine*, and 10, with *little or no debate*. The fact is most significant, but of *what?* It could not be that the subject was of little importance, for the people of this country, as well as those of England, had ever considered it of the greatest importance.

The Constitution was adopted in Federal Convention in Sept., 1787, it was first ratified by Delaware, in Dec., 1787, and, lastly, by Rhode Island, in May, 1790. The second State that ratified it was New York, in July, 1788. During that period the press teemed with letters, essays, and addresses, for and against it. Every material objection to it was taken up and discussed by Madison, Hamilton, and Jay, in a series of papers, which, together, are now known as *The Federalist*. Yet, in them, this clause is mentioned but twice, and by Hamilton, who, in one, says, the Writ is amply confirmed; and, in the other, (No. 84,) he argues that it is secured by the Constitution as well as by a Bill of Rights. That "the practice of arbitrary imprisonment has been, in all ages, the favorite and most formidable instrument of tyranny," and then cites from Blackstone (vol. 1, p. 136) the passage that such imprisonment is more dangerous to liberty than violently to take property or life; but not a word is said about having taken this power from the Legislature. It is true, then, that for some reason, there was very little objection to this clause, and it is *certain* that there was no objection to it on the ground that the power of suspending the privilege was to be exercised by a department of the Government which should not exercise it. Nay, more, as to which of the departments had it, there seems to have been a universal concurrence of opinion.

So objectionable were some parts of the Constitution to the more Democratic part of the members, that some of them either left the Convention itself, or refused to sign it, and afterwards did all they could, both in the State Conventions and elsewhere, to prevent its ratification; among these may, especially, be mentioned, Luther Martin, of Maryland; Yates and Lansing, of New York; Mason and Edmund Randolph, of Virginia, and Gerry, of Massachusetts.

In the State Conventions, the chief objections to it were that it consolidated all the powers of the States and people in the Federal Government; that their rights were at its mercy; that it contained no Bill of Rights; that trial by jury, freedom of speech, freedom from arrest, unless upon a warrant supported by oath, and the prohibition of excessive bail, were not sufficiently provided for; and, indeed, the Constitution was only ratified upon the well understood assurance that these things should all be, as they were immediately afterwards, secured by amendments. There were other objections, too, some of them real, many of them chimerical. Patrick Henry, above all others, was persistent in his objection to it, on the ground that it did not sufficiently fence in and guard the liberty of the people. Was there then no objection to this clause? The answer is, there were two objections. It was objected, 1st. That the privilege ought not to be suspended for any time, or *at all.* 2d. That, at least, the *time* of the suspension ought to have been limited, as it was in the Constitution of Massachusetts, whence it was borrowed; but, it was *universally agreed*, that *Congress alone* had the power to suspend the privilege; and those objections were to entrusting that power even to Congress. It was this universal understanding and supreme consciousness of the fact, that Congress alone had the power to suspend, which accounts for the fact, that neither in the Federal or in any of the State Conventions, was there a question raised as to which department of the Government had the power; and that will now be made evident by the express and recorded resolution of one Convention, and by the declaration of every member of each Convention, who spoke either for or against the clause itself.

In the New York Convention, on July 2, towards the close of the proceedings, it is recorded in 1 Ell. Deb., p. 350, that "The Committee (of the Whole) then proceeded through sections 8, *nine*, (that in question,) and 10, of this article, (first,) and the whole of the next, with little or no debate. As the Secretary read the paragraphs, amendments were made in the order and form hereafter recited. In the paragraph, "Sec. 9. Respecting the privilege of the Habeas Corpus," Mr. TREDWELL moved this amendment: "*Resolved*, That whenever the privilege of Habeas Corpus shall be suspended, such suspension shall, in no case, exceed the term of six months, or until the *next* meeting of the Congress." Thus, assuming that Congress passed the Act at one session, it sought to limit the time, for which they should suspend it, to six months, or till their *next* session. The New York Convention adopted the Constitution; but they prefaced that adoption by a Declaration of Rights, which they declared "cannot be abridged or violated," and "are consistent with the said Constitution;" and one of them is in these words—"That every person restrained of his liberty is entitled to an inquiry into the lawfulness of such restraint, and to a removal thereof if unlawful; and that such inquiry and removal ought not to be denied or delayed, except when, on account of public danger, the CONGRESS shall suspend the privilege of the Writ of Habeas Corpus."

Then followed certain amendments which they had confidence would be—and which they enjoined their Representatives to exert themselves to have—adopted; one of which is in these words, "That the privilege of the Habeas Corpus shall not be suspended for a longer term than six months, or until twenty days after the meeting of the CONGRESS *next* following the *passing* the *Act* for such suspension."

These resolves set the whole question at rest. They express the opinion of Hamilton, Jay, Livingston, Morris, Clinton, and others. They have distinctly declared, in reference to the very clause in question, that it is the *Congress* which has the power to suspend the privilege; and the question now is, were they, who made the Constitution, mistaken, or are those who differ from them mistaken?

To these will now be added the recorded opinions of the makers of the Constitution (and of those who ratified it) in the Conventions of the several States. In reply to a congratulatory address, Mr. Jefferson said: "The Constitution shall be administered by me according to the safe and honest meaning contemplated by the plain understanding of the people at the time of its adoption; a meaning to be found in the explanations of those who advocated, not those who opposed it. These explanations are presented in the publications of the times." And the same sources of explanation are referred to in Mr. Madison's letter to Mr. C. J. Ingersoll, Feb. 22, 1831—4 Elliott's Debates, pp. 414, 446. It was Mr. Tredwell who, in the New York Convention, moved the amendment limiting the time of the suspension. He objected to any suspension, but thought that at least its duration should be limited. He, also, objected to the terms of the clause, which seemed to concede a prior power in the General Government, of which it was but the limitation. On these points he said, (2 Elliott's Debates, p. 399,) " Why is it said that the privilege of the Writ of Habeas Corpus shall not be suspended unless, in cases of rebellion or invasion, the public safety requires it ? What clause in the Constitution, except this very clause itself, gives the *General Government* a power to deprive us of that great privilege, so sacredly secured to us by our State Constitution? Why is it provided that no bill of attainder shall be passed, or that no title of nobility shall be granted? Are there any clauses in the Constitution extending the powers of the General Government to these objects? Some gentlemen say that these, though not necessary, were inserted for greater caution." That is to say, those who defended this Habeas Corpus clause, among others, had justified its insertion, not for the purpose of giving a power, but for greater caution to restrain a power which otherwise might be exercised by the General Government, certainly not by the Executive. No matter, however, about that point; it is clear that Mr. Tredwell, and all who heard him, never questioned but that the power, with or without the clause, belonged to Congress only.

Luther Martin, a delegate from Maryland to the Federal Convention, opposed the ratification of the Constitution on the grounds, among others, that it gave too much power to the General Government, did not sufficiently secure the civil rights of the people, and that it did not prohibit the slave trade. In his address to the Legislature of Maryland, detailing the grounds of his objections, he says :

" By the next paragraph, the *General Government* have a power of suspending the Habeas Corpus Act in cases of rebellion or invasion.

" As the State Governments have a power of suspending the Habeas Corpus Act in those cases, it was said [in the Federal Convention] there could be no reason for giving such a power to the General Government, since, whenever the State which is invaded, or in which an insurrection takes place, finds its safety requires it, it will make use of that power. And it was urged that if you give this power to the General Government, it would be an engine of oppression in its hands; since whenever a State should oppose its views, however arbitrary and unconstitutional, and refuse submission to them, the General Government may declare it to be an act of rebellion, and, suspending the Habeas Corpus Act, may seize upon the persons of those advocates of freedom who have had virtue and resolution enough to excite the opposition, and may imprison them during its pleasure, in the remotest part of the Union; so that a citizen of Georgia might be *bastiled* in the farthest part of New Hampshire, or a citizen of New Hampshire in the farthest extreme of the South, cut off from their family, their friends, and their every connection. These considerations induced me, sir, to give my negative to this clause, also."

Mr. Martin's objection was to any suspension—even by Congress. It had not entered into his imagination that the Executive could claim, or that others would claim for him, this objectionable power.

In the Massachusetts Convention, the Constitution was debated between January 9th and February 6th, 1788. On January 26th, the Journal of the debates records that—

" The paragraph which provides that the privilege of the Writ of Habeas Corpus shall not be suspended unless in cases of rebellion or invasion," was read, when General Thompson asked the President to please to proceed. " We have," said he, " read the book often enough; it is a consistent piece of inconsistency."

Hon. Samuel Adams, in answer to an inquiry of the Hon. Mr. Taylor, said: " That this power given to the *General Government* to suspend this privilege in cases of rebellion and invasion, did not take away the power of the several States," &c.

Dr. Taylor asked, why this darling privilege was not expressed in the same manner it was in the Constitution of Massachusetts? Here he read the latter, and remarked on the difference of expression, and asked, why the *time* was not limited ?

Judge Dana said, "The answer, in part, to the honorable gentleman must be, that the same men did not make both Constitutions; that he did not see the necessity or great benefit of limiting the time." Supposing it had been, as in our Constitution, "not exceeding twelve months," yet, as our Legislature can, so might *the Congress*, continue the suspension of the Writ from time to time, or from year to year. The safest and best restriction, therefore, arises from the nature of the cases in which *Congress* are authorized to exercise that power at all, namely, in those of rebellion or invasion. These are clear and certain terms, facts of public notoriety, and whenever these shall cease to exist, the suspension of the Writ must necessarily cease, also. He thought the citizen had a better security for his privilege of the Writ of Habeas Corpus under the Federal than under the State Constitution, for our Legislature may suspend the Writ as often as they judge "the most urgent and pressing occasions" call for it. He hoped these short observations would satisfy the honorable gentleman's inquiries, otherwise, he should be happy in endeavoring to do it by going more at large into the subject.

Judge Sumner said, that this was a restriction on *Congress*, that the Writ of Habeas Corpus should not be suspended except in cases of rebellion or invasion. The learned Judge then explained the nature of this Writ.

This privilege, he said, is essential to freedom, and, therefore, the power to suspend it is restricted. On the other hand, the State, he said, might be involved in danger; the worst enemy may lay plans to destroy us, and so artfully as to prevent any evidence against him, and might ruin the country without the power to suspend the Writ was thus given. *Congress* have only power to suspend the privilege to persons committed by their authority. A person committed under the authority of the States will still have a right to this Writ.

After the several articles had each been debated, there was a discussion upon them generally, when Mr. Nason said—

"The paragraph that gives *Congress* power to suspend the Writ of Habeas Corpus claims a little attention. This is a great bulwark—a great privilege, indeed. We ought not, therefore, to give it up on any slight pretence. Let us see: how long is it to be suspended? As long as rebellion or invasion shall continue. This is exceeding loose. Why is not the time limited, as is in our Constitution? But, sir, its design would then be defeated. It was the intent, and by it we shall give up one of our greatest privileges."

In the Virginia Convention.—It would be tedious to cite all the passages which assert the power of Congress alone to suspend this privilege. Neither those in favor of, nor those opposed to, the Constitution in a single instance attributed that power to the President. Two passages only will be quoted. Mr. Nicholas, who supported the Constitution, said—" But it is complained that they (the Congress) may suspend our laws. The suspension of the Writ of Habeas Corpus is only to take place in cases of rebellion or invasion. This is necessary in these cases, in every other case *Congress* is restrained from suspending it. In no other case can *they* suspend our laws, and this is a most estimable security.—Virg. Deb., 81.

Mr. Grayson opposed the Constitution ; he said—" The second clause, ninth section, of the first article provided, that the privilege of the Writ, &c. Now, if this restriction had not been here inserted, would not *Congress* have had a right to suspend that great and valuable right ?"—Ib. p. 319, 330, 407 ; see also pages 50, 81, 179, 327.

In 1807, on the occasion of Burr's conspiracy, the Senate of the United States passed a bill to suspend for three months the privilege of the Writ of Habeas Corpus. Among the Senators then present were George Clinton, Timothy Pickering, James A. Bayard, Samuel Smith, William B. Giles, and John Quincy Adams; the latter three brought in the bill.

In the House were John Randolph, Josiah Quincy, Nathaniel Macon, Livingston, Theodore Dwight, Pitkin, Dana, and others, eminent for their learning. The bill was objected to on the grounds that it was bad in principle, dangerous as a precedent, and would be abused in practice if imprisonment at will were intrusted to even the best of Presidents. It was argued that it suspended the personal rights of the citizen, it would place them under a military despotism, it dispensed with the operation of the laws, and that the public safety did not require it—and 113 voted against, and only 19 for it.

That was instantly followed by a bill to further secure the privilege to persons in custody, under the authority of the United States. Its mover, James M. Broome, of Delaware, said, " In ordinary times there was no temptation to transgress the limits of constitutional law ; but in times of turbulence, the formal recognition of rights would be a feeble barrier against the inflamed passions of men in power, whether excited by an intemperate zeal for the supposed welfare of the country, or by the detestable motives of party rancor or individual oppression." The debates are full of the like sentiments. The bill was postponed by a vote of 68 to 50 ; but in the debates on both bills it was unanimously agreed that Congress alone could suspend the privilege ; indeed no man questioned that. See 3 Benton, Ab. Deb., p. 490-542.

Of Judicial Authority.—MARSHALL, Ch. J., said, in 1807, in *ex parte* Bollman, 4 Cranch Rep. 101: " If at any time the public safety should require the suspension of the powers vested by this act in the Courts of the United States, it is for the *Legislature* to say so. That question depends on political considerations on which the Legislature is to decide. Until the Legislative will be expressed, this court can only see its duty, and must obey the laws."

JUDGE STORY, Commentaries on the Constitution of the United States, vol. 3, p. 209 : " Hitherto no suspension of the Writ has ever been authorized by Congress since the establishment of the Constitution. It would seem, as the power is given to *Congress* to suspend the Writ of Habeas Corpus in cases of rebellion or invasion, that the right to judge whether the exigency had arisen, must exclusively belong to that body."

TANEY, Ch. J., in *ex parte* John Merryman : " Merryman was arrested by a military officer, without oath or warrant, and without a proclamation or order of the President suspending the privilege; but he had delegated that power to the officer to be exercised when he should think proper to exercise it. The Chief Justice decided the very point, holding it as hitherto unquestioned by anybody, that Congress alone could suspend the privilege."

WOODBURY J., in Luther *vs.* Borden, 7 Howard 80, assumed it as undoubted, that Congress alone had this power, and says of the arrests in Burr's conspiracy : "And Congress then declined to suspend that Writ * * * although the bill provided it should be done only when one is charged on oath with treason. Such a measure was deemed at best but a species of dictatorship," even when done by Congress.

Of Commentators and Text-writers.—RAWLE on the Constitution, p. 114.—"Of this (requirement of public safety) the Constitution probably intends that the Legislature of the United States shall be the judges, charged as *they* are with the preservation of the United States from both those evils, (rebellion and invasion,) and it seems not unreasonable that this control over the Writ of Habeas Corpus should rest with them."

"We have seen that there is one law, securing the privilege of the Writ of Habeas Corpus, which cannot be suspended even by the *Legislature,* unless in the extreme emergencies of rebellion or invasion."—Walker's introduction to American Law, p. 195-6.

HENRY ST. GEORGE TUCKER'S Commentaries, 1836, vol. 1, p. 42.—Congress alone can suspend the privilege of the Writ of Habeas Corpus. Such an attempt was made during the apprehensions entertained of Col. Burr's designs, but failed."

THEODORE SEDGWICK, in his Commentaries on Statutory and Constitutional Law, (1857,) p. 598, says :

"Practically, as yet, *Congress* has never authorized the suspension of the Writ. It is understood that as the unlimited power (in cases of rebellion or invasion) is vested in Congress, the right to judge of the expediency of the exercise is also vested absolutely in that body."

Smith's Commentaries on Constitutional Law; p. 364.—This author considers "the restrictions laid upon the Legislative power of the Union, under express prohibitions found in the same instrument; and among them is that which forbids the Habeas Corpus to be suspended."

The last Commentary on the Constitution is that of George Ticknor Curtis, of Boston, in the second volume of whose work, published in 1858, he says,—"There now remains to be considered the *restraints* imposed upon the exercise of the power of *Congress* both within the States and in all other places ; some of them relate to special powers, "but others are introduced which apply to the exercise of all the powers of Congress, and are in the nature of limitations upon its general authority as a Government—one of these is embraced in the clause that the privilege of the Writ of Habeas Corpus shall not be suspended," &c.

The only comprehensive treatise on the Writ of Habeas Corpus published in this country is that by Mr. Rolin C. Hurd, of Ohio; and published in 1858. In that work Mr. Hurd says, "Rebellion and invasion are eminently matters of national concern, and charged as Congress is, with the duty of preserving the United States from both these evils; it is fit that it should possess the power to make effectual such measures as it may deem expedient "to suppress them." And he is clearly of opinion that Congress, alone, can suspend the privilege of the Writ.—p. 133.

Of the Judicial Opinions.—Chief Justice Marshall had been a member of the Virginia Convention, which adopted the Constitution. He was intimate with Madison and the other eminent Virginia Statesmen, who aided to prepare it. In the State Convention, itself, he heard it over and over again asserted, and never denied, that Congress alone could suspend the privilege, and he was doubtless perfectly familiar with the history of the clause, itself.

He was Chief Justice when the alleged accomplices of Burr were arrested, and when President Jefferson conceded that he had not the power, and when Congress acted under it, but refused to suspend the privilege. It was at this very time, viz., in 1807, he gave his opinion in *ex parte* Bollman, 4 Cranch. 101. To say that he did not understand the meaning of this clause is, to say the least of it, highly improbable. Judge Story may have used loose and inaccurate expressions, but no man was better informed than he was, as to the history of the Constitution, and in it he failed to find a spark of evidence that the Executive had this power.

Of Chief Justice Taney's decision,—the best vindication is that the eminent men who prepared the Constitution; those who in the several State Conventions discussed this and its other clauses, and who adopted it; the Judges of the Supreme Court who have since considered it; the statesmen who have thence, till 1861, administered the General Government; the several Text-writers, Commentators, and Lawyers who have written upon the Constitution, have all, without a single exception, maintained the position on which he based his judgment.

In conclusion, one topic, though of little weight as an argument, may be noticed; it has been said that the "President has no power that can be abused, except with more danger to himself than to the community;" and that in Mr. Bulwer Lytton's opinion, ours is "the feeblest Executive perhaps ever known in a civilized community."

Is it not plain that the inference from all that is against the President's having the power to suspend the Habeas Corpus? If his power be so limited as to make him "the feeblest Executive ever known," who made him so feeble, but the Federal Convention? It was not by accident that such men as were in it kept power from him; it was by design, and in that is seen another evidence of their intention to withhold from him the prerogative of suspending the peoples' privileges. But if they thus well and wisely withheld so much power from him, has not the *influence* of his office increased, and is it not increasing? When in 1690, the English Crown was settled upon William III., its powers were limited and fixed by law; but, substituting the "President" for the "Crown," the words of a philosophic Englishman are true of the office of the former. "From the time of the Revolution accordingly we may trace in some measure a new order of things; a new principle of authority, which is worthy the attention of all who speculate upon political subjects. Before that period, the friends of liberty dreaded only the direct encroachment of the prerogative. They have since learned to entertain stronger apprehensions of the secret motives of interest which the Executive may hold up to individuals, and by which it may seduce them from the duty which they owe to the public. To what a height in fact, has this influence been raised in all the departments of Government, and how extensively has it pervaded all classes and descriptions of the inhabitants? In the Army, in the Navy, through the Custom Houses, the Post Offices, the Mints, and through a partizan Newspaper press; together with many other offices connected with the distribution of justice, the execution of the laws, and the *corps diplomatique*. With what a powerful charm does it operate in regulating opinions, in healing grievances, in stifling clamors, in quieting the noisy patriot, in extinguishing the most furious opposition.

"It is the great opiate which inspires political courage and lulls reflection; which animates the statesman to despise the resentment of the people; which drowns the memory of his former professions, and deadens, perhaps, the shame and remorse of pulling down the edifice which he had formerly reared."—Millar on Gov., vol. 4, p. 94.

Philadelphia, March 4th, 1862.

www.ingramcontent.com/pod-product-compliance
Lightning Source LLC
Chambersburg PA
CBHW032122080426
42733CB00008B/1025